The Devil Wears Condoms

Author:

Victorya Hubicki

Co-Writer:

Christine Marina Feliciano

Paperback ISBN: 979-8-9914096-1-2

PREFACE:

Allow me to reintroduce myself, my name is Victorya. Most of you know me from my explicit content, viral videos, or from the domestic abuse showcased online via my social media. To my mother, I am a daughter; to some, I am a friend; and to others, I am an inspiration. If you think you know me, think again. I've grown and changed, shaped by all my past experiences and the triumphs I've faced. My transformation has been mind-boggling and inspiring to watch. I am not the same woman I was a year ago; I am flourishing unapologetically in my metamorphosis.

Becoming self-aware and taking accountability has been life changing. Breathing is something we do naturally. When born into the world, we take our first breath; as life begins, we are forced to learn things that go without saying. Most begin unfortunately learning from trauma, forcing their survival skills to kick in. Others learn through love. Love is a skill that involves personalization of your feelings along with effective communication, emotional intelligence, and empathy. It is a diligent balance of give and take; while respecting one's boundaries, emotional flexibility, and empathy; for the other person/people in the equation. Once you practice self-love, boundaries, and limitations, everything in your life starts to set in place. These new bylaws you form apply to everyone. Respecting yourself becomes your limit, not just a fallacy, it's your reality.

As I get older and wiser, I have learnt the importance of balance and stability. Feeding your brain positivity after being fed fast food for years is important. It allows everything else in your life to fall apart or come together.

I have yet to find a permanent solution to this ongoing conundrum.

Drowning in medication is not an acceptable solution, and neither is drowning in alcohol. I will not lie, I am better, but I am still working on a few kinks. I still don't have it all figured out, but who does?

As sick as this sounds, I am glad I went through what I went through; it made me the woman I am today. Accepting my flaws and being grateful for every moment. Some days, I must step out of my body, bask in my fortitude, and be thankful for the abundance I was given. I accept my chosen path even if I have made some wrong turns. It has forced me to awaken the person I was meant to be. That's why you're reading this right now.

This book is my testament, and I am proud of it. It is the start to healing my soul, and I hope it will help others and give them some strength. Everybody goes through shit in life, some people are just better at hiding it than others. I've never been good at hiding things, whether it's emotions or my personal business. My hopes are that anyone reading this absorbs the growth and betterment I have endured thus far. Never give up and keep going. Life goes on and is beautiful; you deserve to enjoy all it has to offer.

CONTENTS

Acknowledgments

Writing this book has been an incredible journey of self-discovery and healing, and I could not have done it alone. I am deeply grateful to everyone who has supported me along the way.

First and foremost, I want to thank my mother, whose unwavering love and support have been my anchor through the toughest times. Your strength and resilience have always inspired me.

To my friends, thank you for standing by me, offering your friendship, and believing in me even when I doubted myself. Your encouragement has been invaluable.

I am also profoundly thankful to my mentors and advisors who guided me, providing wisdom and insight that helped shape this book. Your belief in my vision gave me the confidence to pursue this project wholeheartedly.

A special thanks to my co-writer, whose meticulous attention to detail and dedication helped bring this book to life. Your guidance and support have been crucial in making this book the best it can be.

To everyone who has followed my journey through social media, thank you for your steadfast support and for sharing your own stories with me. Your messages of hope and resilience have been a source of inspiration and strength.

Lastly, I want to acknowledge all the individuals and organizations who have worked tirelessly to support survivors of trauma and domestic abuse. Your efforts are making a difference, and this book is a testament to the power of healing and transformation.

Thank you all from the bottom of my heart. This book is for you, and I hope it brings as much healing and strength to you as it has to me.

CHAPTER 1

Behind the Camera: The Complex World of an Adult Film Star

The allure of an adult film star's world, perceived as effortless and captivating, is a deceptive facade. Contrary to widespread belief, this industry isn't solely about on-camera fucking and climaxing. Trust is the cornerstone of relations. In most cases, it is the real glue that holds relationships together and allows you to move forward with the intimate partners of your choice. It's not just about getting fucked, licked, sucked, and your pussy pounded so hard you can't walk. It's much more than what is shown to the naked eye. Throughout my journey, in my first serious relationship, I believed I had found security—a sense of stability I had long sought. Although I occasionally ventured into scenes with other men, I primarily worked with my partner.

Nonetheless, I'm human, and interactions with other men, both on and off camera, were inevitable. Can you really fault me? Surrounded by the magnetism of these men who were so well endowed, I only saw but never experienced firsthand, only through the clicks of my computer mouse. Hearing other women's genuine pleasure, their bodies in ecstasy, left me envious and hungry for the same attention. I craved an experience leaving my body so satisfied I'd struggle to walk. Thirsty didn't even begin to describe it. I understand why they say temptation is the devil's playground.

The attraction of these encounters stemmed from the visual narrative—the raw expressions of pleasure, you know, women having huge dicks of unimaginable sizes plunging their insides, watching them go in and out of creaming pussies as they screamed for more. A language of its own, captured in the videos and pleasurable expressions. The tantalizing temptation was undeniable, yet the reality behind the scenes wasn't always aligned with this pleasure. The performances and endurance of men on the sets were unlike anything I'd encountered.

This is in staggering contrast with previous experiences where swift climaxes occurred, often under five minutes, were the norm. When my time came, I was ready. My hopes were high, and nothing could stop me from feeling the ecstasy I long craved. Instead, my first on-set encounter felt like I drove my G-Wagon to a quick-service shop, only to have them botch a simple oil change before swiftly sending me off—a complete disappointment and a waste of time. But I still loved porn; I mean, it was making me damn good money, and that alone made me climax.

My first foray into the adult world of pornography was with my then-partner, Daijon. My collaboration with Daijon was sourly focused on the financial benefits our videos may generate on platforms such as OnlyFans and our private Snapchat. Our intimacy was limited to the lens, which was a source of financial advantage. Off-camera, our sexual intimacy felt non-existent, leaving me yearning for genuine connection elsewhere. We started off as a conventional couple, not living together; I worked a 9-to-5 job, living a lifestyle of paycheck to paycheck while studying finance in college. I quickly gained popularity online, and the dynamics transformed, changing me into an income generator.

Inadvertently— the lack of companionship between Daijon and I taught me emotional detachment, numbing my ability to experience pleasure. Pleasure became a calculated commodity, a skill honed over time. However, he wasn't the sole contributor; various relationships shaped and reinforced this pattern, that molded my psyche. Unfortunately, pleasure became synonymous with financial gain rather than personal enjoyment. Filming the "perfect scene" demanded separating emotions from business—a perpetual work in progress. I am not saying I was perfect either; every story has a villain, and you get to decide who it is. The fine line between pleasure and financial gain blurred, convoluting my relationships.

A pivot in my success strategy was the creation of amateur-style porn—a reflection of my early fascination with pornography that transitioned into a full-time occupation. I became an expert at embodying the persona of a "horny, super slutty OnlyFans girl," despite the growing divide between this on-screen identity and my authentic desires, my work life began intruding on my personal life.

The constant doubt—were people drawn to me for myself or my fame? Would I ever find a partner who cherished me for me beyond the shadow of my fame? Was I just a fantasy? Questions like these weighed heavily, prompting extra security measures in public and a continuous sense of vigilance. Distinguishing genuine interest from opportunism became a difficult task. My new lifestyle caused a void in connections. Utilizing sex as a means of survival weathered trust, causing a need for frequent STD testing, and pregnancy scares, which sparked self-reflection on the impact of my choices in relationships and my life's trajectory.

As I share my story and insight into the field of adult filmmaking, I hope you learn about my journey and the sacrifices it requires. An adult film star's schedule is different from societies norms or the structure of a 9-5 work week. Filming begins depending on fan requests or subject matter, sometimes spontaneously, as in my recent encounter in Paris, a trip for leisure. demonstrating the fluidity of this vocation and the various interpretations of the "perfect scene" amongst porn aficionados. The notion that adult entertainment is merely cosmetic ignores the deep layers and intricacies lying beneath every scene, a reality veiled by the screen's surface glamor.

CHAPTER 2

Unveiling the Woman Behind the Screen: The Real Life of an OnlyFans Star

Misconceptions about OnlyFan's personalities are rampant, breeding judgment and assumptions. Our identities are often reduced to mere sexual figures, devoid of personal struggles. Describing my profession as a challenge is an understatement; while I can't say I'm a teacher or a lawyer, I am an empowered entrepreneur, a self-made millionaire. Initially, my career path didn't align with my parents' expectations of me, but my occupational choice allowed me and my family to live a lot more freely.

I've seen the world's luxuries and amassed great financial success, but nothing compares to the primal, satisfying pleasure of an orgasm. Fortunately, sex sells, as does the charm of engaging with a sex worker. From a very young age, my journey with pornography began with an over consumption addiction of porn; it was so bad that my stepdad installed site blockers on my devices. Masturbating multiple times daily—before consistent encounters—was my norm. A girl has needs, and mine always leaned towards climaxing. I suppose I've been passionate about this my whole life.

Growing up fast taught me that my norm wasn't universal; The words of Morticia Addams' resonate with me: "Normal is an illusion. What is normal for the spider is chaos for the fly."

Initially, my parents grappled with disappointment, their confusion apparent in rapid blinks and alarm. They needed to take my newfound career and porn fame all in. Time allowed for optimism, fostering an acceptance of my identity and career path. Yet, beyond the screen lies me, a person with emotions, aspirations, and struggles. Money brings its comforts but solves only some problems. My endeavor is to maintain authenticity, both with myself and my fans.

I've wrestled with my own demons and navigated through others' projections and unfathomable experiences. Depression and trauma are just fragments of the battlefield I've navigated. Focused on personal growth and mental health, I continuously work on myself. Genuine connections are vital to me; my family, friends, and industry experiences have taught me the value of these bonds.

Navigating relationships within this industry is complex. Men often struggle to embrace my profession; external judgments add weight to the burden. Yet, despite these challenges, I hold hope that someone will love and accept me unconditionally for who I am.

Initially, as an Instagram model advertising for brands like Fashionova, where at the time I barely received compensation—often just free clothing; a stark difference from how I am compensated for deals now. Juggling a consignment store job and college expenses, I lived at my parents' house, commuting to West Chester University in a dilapidated Nissan Altima. Unsatisfied with the bare minimum, I met Daijon. I remember him because, Unfortunately, it is hard to forget someone that you fucked on camera for years; if it wasn't for him, my destiny with porn would probably be non-existent. He introduced me to private Snapchat, an avenue that changed my life's path. Private Snapchat brought in more income in hours than a week's work at Style Encore. That's why salt looks like sugar; you won't know what you're getting until you taste it.

The shift to OnlyFans, was inevitable. We could see the financial reward although it posed challenges for me such as hiding it while living with my parents. The rapidly increasing income led me to drop out of college and move into an apartment with Daijon, committing ourselves entirely to OnlyFans. We were propelled by the excitement of newfound wealth—a clear-cut contrast to those who lost everything during the pandemic. With sex, our phones, and the internet, we achieved our dreams.

Before my adult entertainment venture, I dreamed of a business and finance degree. Fate had other plans, leading me down an unconventional path. It's been a rollercoaster ride marked by personal growth, excruciating lessons, and the courage to be authentic. Along this journey, I've faced familial tensions, struggled with my mental health, and navigated complex relationships.

From the industry's incessant scrutiny and criticism on social media a career in adult entertainment can be mentally draining. You are defined in the industry by your earnings, and the pressure to appease demanding fans is relentless. Yet, I strive to maintain authenticity, empowering women to love their bodies and feel confident. You know, Victorya the girl in the Nissan Altima who started with nothing but a dream and an iPhone.

Emerging stronger, I've fortified my sense of self, setting boundaries while upholding my morals and values in all interactions; even though that's not the public opinions on adult stars.

The perception of being a moralless being has its attractions. Still, I prefer to display my intimate skills off-camera, and strangely enough, most men don't like their sexual encounters recorded but like to watch sex occur on camera. Despite misconceptions, OnlyFans is empowering. It's a 24/7 job requiring self-motivation—some days, finding that motivation is daunting.

My fans motivate me by showing support through jacking their dicks to me daily. I know that sounds hard to believe, but it's proven. Ask my accountant. What can I say? I know how to drain a man's balls; it's my specialty and I don't even have to physically be there to do it. I cherish the moments when they recognize me in public. Making a difference matters; however, the pressure to continually provide content weighs on me heavily. OnlyFans permits flexible work hours, enabling me to generate income from anywhere globally. My earnings facilitated world travel and dream purchases, like my beloved car and properties. Public content initially boosted my popularity despite OnlyFans' restrictions on such material.

Accumulating over five million dollars on OnlyFans was a significant milestone, emphasizing that money isn't everything. My consistency and genuine nature earned respect and admiration within the industry. Despite accolades, the industry's incessant demand for more—more explicit content, and more earnings—takes a toll.

Over three years in the business have transformed me and my mentality. Initially, I was accommodating, allowing people to exploit me. But experiences have made me stronger, steering me away from fake industry relationships. The need to compartmentalize every situation and person has become a survival strategy. My kindness often led to exploitation, but my recent relationship with my ex-boyfriend Sheldon taught me crucial lessons—never underestimate someone's affection, especially from someone who sleeps by your side every night (The Devil). As time would have it my relationship with Daijon ended. It was not a happy ending. It was my first industry relationship that ended swaddled in court documents and pain, but I persevered.

Striving to achieve that elusive .01% status on OnlyFans became my goal. My relentless dedication to consistency and authenticity gained industry-wide respect. The payoff was buying my first dream car, a G wagon—a reward for my hard work and dedication. Despite my rigorous work ethic, finding a consistent man to fuck on camera remained a challenge.

Pushing myself while ensuring self-care remains crucial but daunting; but ambition fuels productivity. Finding contentment in daily accomplishments encourages further progress. The absence of a consistent filming partner compounds the challenge, yet my drive still was encouraged. For me, contentment lies in a day well spent meeting all my goals and aspirations.

Change has been a constant throughout my three-year journey on OnlyFans, especially within myself. The woman who started this journey is not the same as I am today. Initially, I was super sweet and kind, but honestly,

I was a bit of a pushover. I'd let people walk all over me, but that is expected from a woman still learning how to navigate the world. But these years have molded me into a stronger person. I've encountered countless fake friends in this industry—girls and even some men who wanted to get close to me for purposes of exploiting my content and my hard work. I really did become a tool for generating revenue, and everyone wanted this tool in their shed.

Learning to distinguish every relationship and situation became a skill. My big heart landed me in trouble one too many times. I was always eager to help others, but who's there when I need it? Who is going to save me when I need to be saved? Often, these were my intimate thoughts that plagued my mind. It's a question that remains unanswered for me. After my breakup with my most recent boyfriend, Sheldon, we will get into his conniving, manipulating, selfish ass throughout this book. I realized that everyone, including the man who cums in your pussy multiple times a day, might not always like you, love you, or even support you. That was an eye-opener for me. The type of eye-opener that keeps your eyes unlatched and puts your already paranoid behavior on a Richter scale. Talk about PTSD (and I am not talking about my Pussy That's so Delicious.)

The industry started valuing me when I shared my earnings and percentage on OnlyFans. The goal here is to hit that elusive 0.01%. I talked about wanting above. I hovered around 0.02% for a long while—making around $150,000 monthly, which was insane. So, I buckled down to hit 0.01%. Unfortunately, we live in a world where people value pockets more than character. It's all about receipts and proof these days, and I had it. But I've earned respect for my sheer work ability and ethics.

I never missed a day sharing videos, responding to messages, or promoting myself—I was the reliable one. And my reward, well it was my financial gains. I indulged myself with everything this life offers, including diamonds, shoes, bags, and any designer or luxury item that caught my eye. Watching the transformation from a seed to a full-fledged garden is incredible. Hard work and dedication paved my path, a dream that started to unravel into reality.

I hold myself to a high standard, but there's nothing like the satisfaction of completing everything on my daily to-do list. But things have become a tad more challenging lately. I no longer have a consistent filming partner who helped with daily tasks and provided support and motivation. I can't depend on anyone else but me. I must succeed; I don't have any other option. Nevertheless, I treat myself by watching a movie or relishing my favorite foods. My ambition to be productive keeps me going, regardless of my circumstances.

My never-ending pursuit is finding contentment in my daily contributions and ticking off my daily goals. Feeling like I've accomplished enough each day keeps me motivated. Despite my trials and tribulations, I know I am destined for greatness. I can feel it in my bones. This feeling is not just surface-level; it's in my soul. What's that saying, it's in me not on me.

CHAPTER 3

Beneath the Surface: Mental Health and Self Awareness

In this industry, the spotlight shines brightly on the glitz and glamour, but behind the scenes, it's a battleground for mental health. It takes an armor-plated mindset to thrive in porn. Your income is intricately tied to your image, and every day, social media acts like a critic, nitpicking on every flaw they can find. Despite learning to brush it off, there are times when those opinions still sting. In this world, worth is often gauged by monetary earnings, and that pressure takes a toll. You find yourself bending over backward, doing things you never thought you would do to maintain the same income. But the fans, they're insatiable. Always craving more content, more consistency, and more performers on screen.

I've never filmed with more than one guy at a time, drawing my boundaries somewhere. The fear of losing subscribers if my content isn't up to par, is a constant worry. Imagine—your image is directly tied to your paycheck. In this industry even men size women up nowadays based on their body, their curves, and their assets, and by assets, I mean money. Over time, I've learned to numb myself to their judgments. I've changed a lot since I started; surgery became a part of my journey and is a must in this industry. Social media warped my perception; surrounded by women that seemed to have stepped out of comic books, shit began to get real.

Money became my coping mechanism—a way to make sense of everything. Financial freedom brought clarity. Amidst all this, I'm grateful for my lifelong friends, those who've stayed true through thick and thin. Porn is a world full of the unknown. You are surrounded by drugs, money, fame, and, at times, violence. It's like living a rock star life without receiving rock star treatment at times, you know, like those D-list celebrities.

You also begin to grapple with your mental health, something I had already had a time with. It has been a lifelong struggle for me. Social media boosted my confidence and gave me moments that affirmed my choice in this profession. The looks on people's faces— be it the bank teller glancing at my monthly deposits or the reaction of my stepdad when he sees my earnings— bring a sense of validation. Again, it's not just about the money; it's about empowerment. Buying a million-dollar house at 23 is quite a feat.

It's ironic how I once priced designer bags at a consignment store, dreaming of affording one, and now, I can walk into any store and buy and bag I want. But it's not just about the material—being recognized and appreciated by strangers feels like validation that I'm doing something right in this life. Yet, there's this persistent misconception that what I do is wrong. There are far worse things in the world than helping people find pleasure; it's empowering. It's given me a sense of confidence and purpose that I never had before. In this world, people respect and look up to me. I've inspired women to embrace themselves, and that feeling is unparalleled.

Growing up, no parent dreams of their child being in

porn, especially on the vast canvas of the internet. The moment my stepfather discovered my Twitter account, labeled under the name "cum slut," was one I'll never forget. The conversation we had was both awkward and comical. I recall walking into his office, seeing the concern on his face, and then the straightforward question, "Are you the cum slut?" I couldn't help but laugh and confirm it was indeed me. It was a tough conversation, especially since I was still living under their roof while filming the content. My stepdad, rooted in a culture, valuing education, wanted me to finish college.

But the amount I made in a month surpassed what many earned in years. Our relationship wasn't the best, and my unresolved issues with my biological father made it harder to bridge that gap. However, I hope he understands my choices and as a testament to how we live now. There's more to my story than meets the eye. Yeah, I'll be honest, I've fought with what people call "daddy issues." Growing up without my father affected a lot of things in my life, especially my relationships with men. I should have included this guidance, the paternal support you see on TV. I didn't have that firsthand experience of seeing how a man should treat his woman or how they build a solid relationship.

My stepfather was good to my mom, but it wasn't the same, especially since I didn't witness it all the time. People might joke about it, but it's deeper than that. Not having a man around to steer me in the right direction and distinguish right from wrong has left me trying to fix broken people in my life, and I had to learn to stop doing that.

Having a father might not have changed everything

because I know plenty of only fan girls with their fathers around. They still do what they do. But deep inside, I can't help but wonder how different things could have been with my dad in the picture. It's sad when people start speculating and making up stories about why someone behaves in a certain way. To me, that's just bullshit. We've got to own up to our stuff, recognize it for what it is, and not lean on it as an excuse or crutch. It might contribute to certain events or situations, but it doesn't define who I am, who I will be, or who I want to be. I'm learning and evolving every single day; it's a process. I am unapologetic in my evolution, and you should be, too.

I take pride in supporting my stepdad and mom and younger sister. They've seen my growth and my commitment. It took some time for them to accept it, you know? Leaving home at a young age and stepping into a world where we weren't used to that kind of money or success was a shift. But they've come around, respecting my drive to chase a dream. A dream that some may consider a nightmare. I remember growing up in a two-bedroom apartment with my grandparents, cousin, and aunt. I'm grateful for certain experiences that humbled me. Sacrificing everything for this can be challenging. People assume it's a breeze to put yourself on the internet, but it's not. It affects every relationship in your life. Sadly, many men struggle to take women in this industry seriously. It's like they're insecure, just as broken as they claim women to be. It's tough, but I'm learning to navigate it all, one step at a time. I may need to catch up on the way, but I know my destination.

CHAPTER 4

The Tangled Web of Love: The Start of a Tumultuous Relationship Revealed

Here's where it gets good. You have learned about my start in this industry, the vial the industry has over it, and where I am presently. Now let's talk about Sheldon, the bastard I mentioned earlier and what I have overcome; the relationship that sparked this book. I met Sheldon through my ex-friend named Sophia, a backstabbing ass cunt. I would tell you more about her but that's for volume II. It was late, and we ended up at Sheldon's house after a night out. From the get-go, Sheldon spun tales about owning businesses in the Dominican Republic, his properties, and even a boat. His words painted an impressive picture, and I bought into it, thinking he had everything together. It seemed like a significant shift from my previous relationship, where financial stability was a struggle, or we had to build together. I was excited.

The thing is, Sheldon was a master manipulator. He could make you believe in a lifestyle he didn't live himself; it was eerie. Imagine meeting someone who is broke but makes you believe they're loaded with properties and wealth. He had roommates but portrayed them as helpers for his house and boat. He even made up a story about how he had to use a business to purchase a new property in Surfside (Florida), stating that he was a black man, and they were racist. I wish what I just divulged was made up. I should have seen the red flags, but I was smitten.

I was 21 when I met him. You know, the time in your life when your mind's a bit hazy, you tend to trust anything you hear, and you're just outright naive. I trusted this 34-year-old man who introduced me to his world on his beautiful boat in sunny Miami. Little did I know this boat ride embarked me on a journey to Hell.

He was quite the actor if I say so myself. If scamming did not work, he really should consider acting in the future. One night turned into three long years; in case you don't know, that is 156 weeks, 1095 days, and 26,280 hours. Time flies when you're being mentally and physically abused, I guess. We ended up filming content, and things got intimate—not just once, but twice. We filmed it; I also must confess I still masturbate to those videos sometimes. Hear me out; it is not that easy to forget someone you were fucking three times a day consistently. I was happy, finally a consistent content partner. It felt different and liberating, especially compared to my previous relationship, where sex felt mechanical and empty. How could something so wrong feel so right?

Suddenly, we were inseparable. I got an apartment in Miami, and Sheldon moved in, claiming it was a privilege for me. His sense of entitlement was odd, and deep down, I sensed he was selling himself a delusional reality. He started with what I know now to be love bombing— showing immense affection and support early on. Looking back, the red flags were glaring, but then, it felt like genuine love, almost a reward after my previous toxic relationship. Boy was I wrong. I was confusing disrespect at the time with love and honor. I wanted it to work badly; it was like I had a veil over my head and couldn't see anything. I had never really been a spiritual person before this relationship. It felt like spiritual warfare; I was fighting a battle I did not know existed; woe is me.

Things went downhill slowly. Sheldon was supposed to help with my OnlyFans and my finances, but it turned into a mess. We weren't exclusive, but he didn't address it directly when he found out about me working with others. He'd say things like, "I wanted to see how far you'd go." He didn't ask for money initially, but things shifted abruptly. He transformed from someone sweet to a completely different person. It got worse, but I was hooked on the love bombing, addicted to the rollercoaster of emotions.

Something that I now know is a trait of a narcissist. He got a kick from watching me suffer; he enjoyed watching me cry; I could tell there was no mercy behind those evil eyes. Those eyes that once made me feel so safe and warm. To this day, I still don't understand. Some things aren't meant to be understood; they are meant to be forgotten. But how can I forget? The image of his brown eyes shadowing his soulless body still lingers in my mind to this day.

It became traumatic for both of us. Sheldon had this love bombing tactic, showering attention, making me feel incredible, then withdrawing it suddenly, leaving me craving that initial high. He shifted the dynamics as time passed, hinting at needing money for our collaborations. Meanwhile, I was dealing with legal issues with my ex, finding solace in Sheldon, unaware he was gathering information to use against me. I started to think that this was my karma. You know, for all my infidelity in my previous relationship with Daijon. What comes around goes around, which is a part of nature I respect.

I craved companionship, the unity of a partnership that felt like a constant, an unwavering presence—something authentic in a world so fake and vile. That's what he portrayed, and that's what I bought into. His words were honeyed promises of undivided attention. He professed to derive his livelihood from property, allowing him to dedicate every moment to me. Gradually, the facade cracked. It began subtly, whispers of aggression and disrespectful undertones.

He maintained his place, occasionally visiting, yet I was footing the bills for his residence, unknowingly ensnared in his trap. He chose his moment to reveal his true colors, transforming from a lover to a manipulator, a cruel enactor of abuse. What was once admiration twisted into envy and malice, his demeanor shifting into a calculated cruelty. His abuse was not confined to closed doors; it spilled into the open, humiliating and disrespecting me in front of friends and family. Their confusion mirrored my own, wondering why I allowed such treatment. I constantly made excuses for him, blaming myself and even excusing his physical abuse because I believed he was "correcting" my behavior. But it got to a point where I could not hide the bruises and swollen eyes any longer; the pain in my face said it all.

Confirmation of his sinister practices came later—a revelation that he resorted to black magic and voodoo to tether me to him, manipulating me into financial servitude. Finding out he took a pair of my used underwear to do work on me. It was a surreal awakening, acknowledging how deeply entangled I had become, lost to a false version of him. It wasn't just me he ensnared; others fell victim to his manipulation and abuse. The trauma wrought a selective amnesia in me, blotting out the darkest moments and leaving voids in my recollections. My brain sought refuge, sheltering me from the worst memories. He would gaslight me and break me down almost daily, I lost track of who I was, and at one point, I even lost the motivation to keep on living.

The relationship took a sharp turn entangling my professional endeavors, a shift marked by his refusal to communicate honestly. Instead, he viewed me as a source of financial gain, risking my life to exert control. He subjected me to horrifying instances of physical harm, choking me and brandishing loaded weapons to taunt me with. Having a loaded gun held to my head became common, and I started hoping he would pull the trigger. His birthday celebration, financed by yours truly, spiraled into toxicity, marred by infidelity and manipulation.

Once again, my desperate attempts to appease him ended in despair, with me facing mental and physical anguish. Caught in a web of deceit, I endured, hiding the truth behind my bruises and fabricating tales to veil the horrors I faced. Attempts to help were rebuffed, as I remained under his spell, trapped in a world of his creation, losing myself. Initially, I believed in an idyllic harmony, a portrait painted with his apparent devotion.

He embraced chores, tended to my dogs, and seamlessly shared a life. But this harmony deteriorated, spiraling into a toxic bitterness. The man beside me each night, sharing intimacy and whispered secrets, was a masterful chameleon—a deception deserving of an Oscar. His counterfeit affection clashed with an unsettling disdain, shattering my perceptions. His elaborate facade made me question his true self's essence and mine.

He lived behind a mask, performing a perpetual act dictated by insecurities and discontent. His portrayal was ingrained in an unalterable identity. Even when faced with evidence contradicting his lies, he clung to them with a tenacity that repulsed me. I doubted my purpose and my value and even questioned God. It felt wrong for someone as fortunate as me to doubt the divine. What a sin. I hope God can forgive me.

I regretted not seeing through his facade earlier. Love, or what I thought was love, became an obsession tied to manipulation and dark enchantments. The toxicity became all I knew; it became a way of living, and nothing else felt right. Memories blurred, casting shadows on once-cherished moments. Naively, I believed our bond was genuine, blind to his hidden motives—envy, jealousy, and a sinister intent to sabotage my life. His covert rivalry was incomprehensible, a battle concealed behind affectionate gestures.

The aftermath forced lessons amidst the chaos— lessons in fiscal prudence, shifts in perspective, and newfound self-awareness. Pain unraveled layers of vulnerability rooted in my upbringing. When I met his family, I understood how he became this way, your own blood can be your biggest enemy and your competition. I learned that some people were raised off love and others' survival. His whole life has been a survival mechanism; he never experienced love; how was he supposed to give it to me!

Or maybe this is me just trying to make excuses for him; Oh no, here we go again. His scars mirrored a troubled past, void of genuine affection, sculpting him into a hollow reflection of humanity. Empathy clashed with rage, a confusion I grappled with during my healing journey. Amid darkness, flickers of tenderness sustained hope. Conversations under the stars, dreams of a future together—they pierced this bleak narrative. His tales of encounters with spirits hinted at an obscured kindness. "Sorry for putting my hands on you, Bubba" (We used to call each other Bubba). I feel bad for people like him; they are soulless, empty, dark, and have wasted potential. Even in his darkest moments, his apologies rang sincere, clouding my judgment and entangling my heart. Shared experiences formed a complex web, weaving doubts about leaving him. He preyed on me and my good heart like a lion hunting for dinner after a severe drought.

Acknowledging my emotional volatility, I confronted the gut-wrenching betrayal of his hidden truths. His apologies remained, but the core of his actions remained unchanged—an evil that's unspeakable. Like they say, I let him do what he wanted to do so I could see and know the truth about what he'd rather do versus telling me a lie about what he wanted to do.

CHAPTER 5

Ironclad

Our relationship resembled a theatrical production, roles concealing our true selves. Despite enduring cruelty, I clung to the belief that goodness existed within him despite the chaos. I left Daijon and our theatrical relationship to join the circus with Sheldon; I was the clown.

We were characterized by phases of happiness then deep sadness shadows that lingered on both of us, leaving wounds that demanded time for recovery. Three years — a timeline encapsulating the peaks of love and the troughs of manipulation, deceit, and abuse both mentally and financially. Was I the problem? Why was I stuck to this man? Was our relationship ironclad, or was I warped in vulnerability and comfort. You know, the Irish idiom, "better the devil you know than the devil you don't. The irony lies in the preference; I still don't know that man.

In the early stages of our story, he showered me with an excess of attention, a phenomenon that I now know is recognized as love bombing. Of course, love bombing worked on me; who wouldn't fall in love with me after a few days. Unbeknownst to me, beneath the veneer of affection lurked a more sinister purpose. Love bombing acted as the cover strategy to induce euphoria through the release of happy hormones—dopamine, norepinephrine, serotonin, and oxytocin. Yet, as swiftly as it commenced, the enchantment was shattered, and the ambiance transformed. True colors surfaced, unraveling a distorted reality. Have you ever been accused of being irrational or delusional about something despite the certainty that you were not? It's akin to the world perceiving one reality while you find yourself in an alternate dimension. Sheldon's mastery of gaslighting was truly remarkable. His skills were so adept that one evening, as I stood in the shower and the water refused to turn hot, my curiosity led me to inquire about the issue with Sheldon, the presumed authority in the house. He responded, "The water is not getting hot because we have been arguing so much. You are bringing bad spirits into our home, and now weird things will suddenly occur." Surprisingly, our home had no disgruntled spirits, harboring animosity toward us and deterring us from enjoying warm showers. Sheldon had simply switched off the water heater; what a deceitful bastard. He could not cover his bullshit up as easily anymore, so he resulted in delusional tactics.

A subtle expectation for monetary contributions seeped into our narrative. He could not afford to be subtle anymore with his need to have access to my funds. Simultaneously his request became entitlement, reminders of a prior relationship lingered—a legal battle that added complexity to my already intertwined emotional landscape.

Sheldon provided an illusion of stability and security, a reassuring presence in my troubled life. He was present, tending to my needs and desires. I now realize that the illusion of stability provided a false sense of what I wanted in a man, ushering me into an impending storm. I'm not to blame; You know, it wasn't me; it was the shitty person that manipulated me. The devil himself, Sheldon.

His shift was metamorphic, he went from kindness to aggression, admiration to envy. His horns emerged, and the once gentle gaze in his eyes transformed into malice, assault, and deception. He has all the prominent ingredients that make up the devil. The descent into abuse was gradual, almost insidious. Aggression, disrespect, and humiliation spilled not only into private moments but also tainted my connections with friends. I got tired; how can I allow someone beneath me to treat me this way. I am Victorya I am who a lot of people would kill to be. Here I stand, a millionaire putting up with a situation that constantly brought life-ending thoughts to me.

His calculated maneuvers were unnerving. The earlier absence of warning signs was a deliberate ploy. You see, I get it now. It's all coming to me. He was strategic in his silence, biding his entanglement to me. Financial responsibilities shifted, and aggression escalated. Rent payments became an unwitting burden, unveiling Sheldon's true nature through acts of disrespect and cruelty. The man isn't really shit or has shit, and baby, it started to show.

The realization struck like a wave, submerging me in the shocking truth that I wasn't the solitary victim of his schemes. The trauma, manipulation, and deceit were orchestrated with precision. The aftermath left me grappling with memories blanketed by memory loss—a defense mechanism adopted by my mind to shield me from my past horrors.

Spirituality emerged as my sanctuary, offering a route to

healing from wounds inflicted by Daijon, now exacerbated by Sheldon. My time with him was marked by turmoil, and my pursuit of solace in a new relationship inadvertently carried the weight of unresolved past traumas.

A pivotal moment unfolded during a trip to Columbia—a celebration that transformed into a nightmare. An illustration of my destain for him led me to compensate other women just to sexually satisfy him, and not just one but multiple women. This was pivotal because it illustrates how bad I just wanted him to be happy, satisfied and love me. **Don't worry; the devil wears condoms.** He was good at protecting himself just not protecting me. Unfortunately, I couldn't write these elaborate splurges off on my taxes but please know that this man had a compensated career with absolutely no benefits earned by me. Manipulation, infidelity, and physical abuse stained the occasion. The toxicity of our relationship reached its peak, and my desperate attempts to salvage happiness were met with violence.

Scars, once concealed by falsehoods, became visible. The mental toll was excruciating. The once-potent spell began to wane, and my cry for help echoed unanswered as the entwined web tightened, leaving me lost in his false reality.

Moving blindly through our relationship marked by scars, unhealing, and newfound awareness. Each chapter unfolds lessons—a painful but essential exploration of self. The shadows may endure, but with each step, I strive to reveal the light that lies beyond. The truth will always set you free.

CHAPTER 6

Finding Myself Amidst the Storm: A Journey Through Passion and Self-Discovery

The impact of passion, in the context of my relationship with Sheldon, reshaped the very fabric of my identity. In the whirlwind of our connection, I found myself teetered on the edge, almost sacrificing the essence of who I was and the woman I wanted to become.

Section 1: "My House, My Identity, What He Tried to Take from Me"

My home, a testament to my dedication and perseverance, reflected my unwavering commitment to my craft, ambition, and rewards. Every renovation, meticulously chosen detail, manifested my love and determination to want and have a better life and to keep building and improving myself. You know that euphoric feeling you get when you achieve something you've long sought, a feeling many yearn for. This was the beginning of Sheldon's ridiculous request. Access to my hard-earned money was not enough. The most absurd thing was for me to add him to the deed of my home. I remember a specific incident when we were in the car, and he was driving; he proceeded to ask me if I was going to put his name on the deed, and when I told him no, he transformed.

His face changed, and his body language spoke for his

feelings. He punched the dashboard hard; I was just glad it wasn't my face or stomach this time. Sheldon's relentless push to have his name associated with my property and nearly swayed me to do so is evidence of how deeply I had fallen for him or that he thought I had fallen. While his encouragement prompted the purchase of my new house, that did not give him the right to own any portion of it. He is Lucifer himself; he will give you what you want, but in return, he will take it all back, including your soul. The heart of the house beat solely to my tune. This was my accomplishment, not his. Every aspect, from financial investment to complex decor, bore the mark of my dedication.

Section 2: "A Fragile Balancing Act"

In a fleeting moment fueled by love and driven by the fear of losing him, I entertained the idea of intertwining Sheldon's name with my home. I harbored the naive belief that adding my property ownership to his name might mend our fractured relationship, hoping it would quell our conflicts and transform his treatment of me. It was like hoping that, as a caterpillar, our relationship would blossom into a beautiful butterfly. But that vulnerable decision only invited further disrespect, eroding my sense of self confidence.

Section 3: "A Disparity in Finance"

I felt bad for not putting his name on my home, so I entertained and reluctantly put Sheldon's name on my bank account while mine remained absent from his. The imbalance, despite my hope for a better relationship, troubled me deeply. The notion of such financial intertwining felt unjust and inherently unfair. It dawned on me: no sensible person would interlace their financial security with someone who wielded disrespect and manipulation. Like the prolific Charles Bukowski said, "Find what you love and let it kill you." I was allowing my love for Sheldon to possibly kill me.

Each decision, each wavering moment unveiled the gravity of the situation. It was a journey of uncertainty, where the lines between love and self-preservation blurred. Yet, these challenges became the foundation of my evolution—a journey toward rediscovering my autonomy and self-worth between the loud storms of passion.

Section 4: "Balance in the Tumult of Passion and Self-Discovery"

Balance, an elusive pursuit, holds immense power. It's a simple word, yet its grasp and frugality are profound, especially when driven by passion. Discipline becomes the linchpin in cultivating and preserving balance. Finding equilibrium within a committed relationship in the adult entertainment industry is advantageous, offering stability amidst the industry's complexities. This is why most women find it hard to let go. Yet, such dependence on a singular person can also lead to pitfalls, forging an overreliance that blurs boundaries. I learned that the only person I can depend on is myself.

From a female perspective, seeking a partner who fosters growth without judgment becomes crucial. You see, my mind played tricks on me. I did not feel worthy; as I stated before, I thought he loved me and was correcting my bad habits. Building a foundation rooted in mutual acceptance and growth is paramount. You feel like you have hit the jackpot as a woman in Porn when you find someone to "love" you. particularly in an environment like OnlyFans, where collaboration is akin to a team effort. My relationship with Sheldon embraced this balance. The comfort and trust I thought we shared, both on and off-camera, indicated a harmonious coexistence. Why did I not realize my life was far from that?

Working in this industry presents a different kind of juggling act compared to traditional 9-to-5 jobs. The relentless pursuit of a career amid extensive hours sacrifices many personal aspects. Martyr becomes the norm—time, money, and even affection is tendered in exchange for professional dedication. However, identifying genuine wants and needs amid these disadvantages is crucial, guiding the path toward something more substantial.

The coil of love and career paths presents challenges in professional pursuits and passionate endeavors. Unhealthy offsets emerge when comfort in a relationship impedes creativity and growth. I lost almost all motivation and drive. our aspirations were not the same anymore. His true self had arrived.

The impact of passion in my relationship with Sheldon resonated deeply. I teetered on the verge of losing myself and my possessions—home, car, and career. My house became a battleground where Sheldon relentlessly sought inclusion. The house symbolized my efforts and investments, yet Sheldon's persistence nearly convinced me otherwise. Moments of contemplation, born from love and fear, only plunged me deeper into a cycle of disrespect and broken compromises.

Within these challenges, self-awareness emerged as the

anchor to my personal growth. I was acquiring knowledge from experiences with Sheldon. These experiences highlighted the depth of self-understanding and the importance of being accepted for one's true self in a relationship. The quest for authenticity and an unwavering commitment to personal boundaries became vital. I have never been good at drawing boundaries or lines; that may be where I went wrong.

Reflecting on past experiences, particularly my pregnancies, revealed moments of profound vulnerability and a broken heart. In my pursuit of self-awareness, I acknowledge my imperfections and recognize the opposition between victimhood and survival. Taking accountability for my actions becomes paramount, recognizing that missteps shouldn't define the path of one's life. I don't mind falling; I promised myself to keep getting back up.

Establishing boundaries and fostering respect began to give me the strength I needed. Self-respect and self-love pushed me into the boundaries I began to stand on; paving the way for identifying personal needs and desires versus what was just lust. This journey, encapsulated within these pages, seeks to unravel my humanity, a piece of me woven from triumphs and regrets.

I want to connect with you all by sharing these deep, intimate moments with my audience, showcasing the human beneath the veneer of social media's glamour. I will allow you to navigate my story, by sharing my truth. My career and personal life, revealing the complexities of my trauma, healing, and self-discovery. When watering, the grass will be greener; just remember to pay the bill.

CHAPTER 7

Unveiling the Truth

"But who prays for Satan? Who, in eighteen centuries, has had the common humanity to pray for the one sinner that needed it most?" - Mark Twain

In the unraveling story of my relationship with Sheldon, the signs of betrayal were always present, lingering like a shadow that refused to fade. Intuition had been my constant companion, a gut-wrenching feeling that whispered secrets of infidelity, yet I lacked the concrete evidence to confront him. Sheldon, a master of denial, would evade the truth until the bitter end, perpetuating a narrative where I became the accused, the liar, and the problem. Wait, aren't those the traits of all narcissists?

His deceit extended beyond emotional betrayal; he manipulated my finances, extracting money as a twisted punishment for perceived wrongs. Gaslighting became his art, leaving me in a perpetual state of doubt about my own reality. The breaking point arrived on a fateful night, a culmination of arguments and spiritual turmoil that cast a dark cloud over our relationship.

During our heated exchange, Sheldon revealed a disturbing encounter, claiming to have witnessed a demonic entity clutching my lifeless form in a closet. The terror on his face mirrored my fear, prompting me to confide in my close friend and assistant, Rob. Rob, how can I express my gratitude to you? You guided me toward a cleansing ritual that would reshape the path of my life. The purification process unearthed profound revelations, and I could sense my spiritual guides actively at work. Within 48 hours of my cleansing, my world began to unravel. Suddenly, I had the proof I needed all along. No, I was not crazy. My instincts were right.

You know that old saying, "What doesn't come out in the wash comes out in the rinse." My cleanse rinsed me. Sarah, one of Sheldon's friends, had played a sinister role in orchestrating his infidelity. Ladies, if you want to know if your man is cheating, ask his "female friends" They know everything, and they probably fuck on the side. A shoulder to cry on becomes a dick to ride on. Sarah's revelations provided the conclusive proof I had long sought. The weight of the deceit lifted, and clarity washed over me like a cleansing tide. What I discovered within those hidden recesses would shatter the illusions I had clung to for three turbulent years of pain, love, and fear. Despite returning home with an unsettled feeling, a few hours after my cleanse, something enticed me to enter my guest bedroom and peek into the closet.

There, two phones secured in a zip-lock bag were ironically lying in plain sight, revealing a trove of evidence that empowered me to break free. As I sifted through the messages and calls, the truth unfolded. Unlocking the phones left me anxious, but upon doing so, I discovered screenshots and videos featuring an ex-girlfriend I was unaware of.

 I reached out to her on Instagram, and coincidentally, Sheldon's Ex was with Sarah that day. Eventually, Sarah called me, reaching a breaking point with the constant back-and-forth between myself and his Ex. She decided to lay everything bare, confessing that Sheldon had disclosed that I was one of his girlfriends who "paid" him. Astonishingly, he cautioned her not to jeopardize this arrangement for him. Sarah came from a lower socioeconomic background, just like Sheldon. She revealed that Sheldon occasionally compensated her for procuring discounted services from sex workers for him, which I guess was part of her reasoning for participating in such sinister acts. We all know that man never wanted to pay full price for anything, evidently that included pussy.

I found myself facing a planned trip the following day with Sheldon, funded by yours truly. Finally, the chains that had bound us began to loosen, and I felt a liberating sense of freedom pursuing me. The upcoming trip carried a hefty price tag, and with a resolve not to squander any more of my hard-earned money, I pressed on, determined to see it through.

What was meant to be a beautiful getaway turned into a psych ward of affairs. Surrounded by the awe-inspiring beauty of the landscape, the two-hour drive to our Villa in the Dominican Republic from the airport felt like swallowing the pits from peaches — those with deep ridges that imprint an unpleasant taste lingering on the palate.

As we embarked on the journey, the blaring music within the confines of the car served as a mere backdrop to the ominous thoughts racing through my mind. Despite its volume, the melodies seemed to move slowly, drowned out by the dark thoughts plaguing my mind. The physical pain I experienced mirrored the dissonance within, starkly contrasting the captivating beauty that enveloped us. At that moment, I felt as though I had descended into my own personal Hell. Arriving at the Villa was no short of punishment; we fought every aching, waking hour, and no pun was intended. He remained steadfast in his deceit, confidently clinging to his lies even when presented with evidence.

He stated that Sarah was simply "jealous" of our relationship, and she was lying. Upon reaching our shared suite, the intensity of the physical violence escalated. His grip around my fragile neck tightened so severely that I blacked out for 10 seconds, convinced I was on the brink of death. In that harrowing moment, I recognized it as God's final warning—a sharp reminder that the next instance could mean death for me. Numerous scars from past plastic surgeries adorned my skin and concealing them had never crossed my mind; shit, I was proud of them.

The relentless abuse from this man left me with no choice. For the first time in my life, body makeup became an essential addition to my daily routine, a staple in my makeup bag. I highly recommend Fenty Beauty's blurring skin tint for its effectiveness and value; it helped me cover my scars. My usual makeup routine extended as I meticulously applied body foundation all over to mask the bruises and marks inflicted by the severity of the abuse to prevent loved ones from asking too many questions.

Returning home from our barbaric "vacation," I discovered the audacity of Sheldon's actions - someone had invaded my sanctuary, packed not only his belongings but also stole some of mine. The audacious act left me flabbergasted but also marked the end of a three-year ordeal. I felt free somehow but very sad. Did I want him to stay and beg for my love, or did Sheldon's leaving give me the courage to face reality?

I was raised catholic; my grandfather made me pray every night before bed, asking God to forgive me for my sins and protect me from evil. I hope God will forgive Sheldon for his sins because I sure won't. How do I find the strength to forgive someone when the consequences of their actions have led me to a lifelong need for therapy?

My therapist is well-off, and I am her sole client in this challenging journey. Does anyone have the phone numbers of Blue Cross and Blue Shield? Also, which healthcare plans have the best coverage for therapists with low deductibles? I'm not asking for a friend. Clearly, I'm asking for myself.

With newfound strength and the undeniable truth, I severed the toxic ties that bound me to Sheldon. Clarity emerged; the psychological locks were destroyed. Revealing a clearer path forward, the journey towards healing and self-discovery began.

CHAPTER 8

"The Chronicles of Resilience: A Journey of Healing"

Section 1: My House, The Battlefield of What Was Once Home

A war zone ravaged by the conflict is now a testament to resilience and restoration. How will I do this now? How do I keep from falling apart? The visions of moments past kept creeping in my path. Memories linger within its walls, haunting me with visions of past traumas. The driveway, once a site of violent outbursts, now echoes with the remnants of abuse. Once a sanctuary of love, the bedroom now feels like a facade of make-believe, tainted by the illusions of intimacy. Even the couch, witness to countless arguments, bears the weight of the war I continuously fight to win. My new reality comes with acceptance; how does that serenity prayer go? "God grant me the serenity to accept the things I cannot change, the courage to change the things that I can, and the wisdom to know the difference...."

But as I navigate the familiar corridors of my home, I realize that the battleground lies not in physical space but within my mind. Every simple action, like unlocking the front door, triggers my PTSD, flooding me with memories of past torment. The trauma seeps through the walls, a constant reminder of the pain I've endured. Despite parting ways with the source of my anguish, the battle between heart and mind rages on.

Then, a shift occurs. A sense of liberation washes over me like a weight lifted from my shoulders. It's as if I've shed 170 pounds of emotional baggage, finally feeling unburdened and free. As my birthday approaches, nostalgia creeps in, reminding me of the love I've longed to receive. But amid the romanticized memories, I find clarity—the realization that true liberation comes from detaching from emotions and embracing rationality. I began to think with my brain and not feel with my heart. Look at me growing up and using discernment. Unfortunately, swimming in regret is not cardio.

Section 2: A King-Size Bed for One

With the dawn of a new day comes the stark reality of my empty bed. The urge to succumb to despair is strong, but I must rise and face the day. My bed is now a symbol of me standing on BUSINESS. As I gather my belongings, I prepare myself for the challenges ahead. I refuse to allow just any man to lay next to me after experiencing Sheldon. Fuck, my therapist was right; I am traumatized. It's time for me to turn this trauma into power, purpose, and profit. You know I'm one hustling ass bitch.

During the mutiny, I find myself thrust into unexpected events. Despite my pain, I'm called upon to fulfill obligations, masking my trauma behind layers of my Fenty foundation and forced smiles. My journey unfolds as a tale of empowerment. The worst part was navigating the world's reaction on social media, where pain is often turned into entertainment. The harsh lesson I learned was the need for privacy; not every battle should be fought in the public eye. The irony is not lost on me as I disguise my scars with special effects, both physical and emotional. Most of the world fakes a smile on social media, portraying only their success, although showing the world one of my biggest failures by exposing Sheldon left me vulnerable; I'm glad I did it.

Section 3: The Show Must Go On

Reflecting on my journey, I see the profound growth I've undergone. Despite the darkness that once consumed me, I stand tall, a testament to my resilience. My evolution is palpable, captured in the transition from adolescence to adulthood, from victim to survivor. The bank does not care what you categorize yourself as; the mortgage must be paid. Bills tell you, you are an adult, even though emotions make you want to return to childhood. O, what would I give to be a child again?

Moving to Miami marked a pivotal chapter in my journey, challenging me to confront my fears and embrace change. The contrast between my small-town upbringing and the bustling city life forced me to adapt, shaping me into the person I am today. I am so grateful for many things; it's so wild how life ebbs and flows. I'm learning to enjoy each moment daily, thanking God for all my successes and failures. My experiences, though at times breaking my spirit, have also fixed my vision. Having entrusted my life to it, I've learned to see through evil and emerged stronger on the other side. These traumatic experiences have reshaped my perspective, making me more emotionally intelligent and adept at understanding others.

Section 4: Finding Strength in Sorrow

Through self-discovery and healing, I've learned to navigate the complexities of life with grace and resilience. As I continue my journey, I carry the lessons learned from my past. My experiences have taught me the importance of self-love, resilience, and embracing imperfection. Though the road ahead may be uncertain, I face it with courage and conviction, knowing that every challenge is an opportunity for growth.

The chronicles of my resilience serve as a marker of hope for those facing their battles. Through authenticity and vulnerability, I hope to inspire others to embrace their struggles and triumph over adversity. For in the darkness, there is always light; in the depths of despair, there is always hope.

Self-awareness, the foundation of personal and professional growth, emerged as a pivotal lesson from my relationship with Sheldon. Years of companionship—sharing meals, a bed, and everyday life—I discovered the irony of not knowing this person. One of the hardest pills to swallow is realizing my enemy was the same person that lays next to me, holding me at night, sick and twisted, right? Just wait. It gets worse. The revelation underscored the importance of mental stability, prompting me to reevaluate who I was and what I allowed. Realization began to dawn on me. Genuine love accepts one as they are. I sought a partner who embraced me authentically, propelling me toward a positive future while respecting my essence.

I knew this was the end. I had to face reality, and that reality would be the only thing that could save me. It got to a point where the painkillers I was taking daily couldn't mask the pain I was experiencing any longer. My salvation meant something to me. Understanding personal desires and boundaries became imperative. Recognizing what suits, me and what I deserve facilitated a forward journey, enabling an authentic life with confident assertions of what aligns with my aspirations needed to be my new focus.

Passion, a realm primarily explored through work, held sway in my life. Yet, in the dept of a breakup with Sheldon, a moment of reckless abandonment questioned the essence of my emotions—was it rage, anger, or a misplaced manifestation of passion? The realization shook me. A woman of my stature and independence pondering such erratic actions screamed self-reflection. Devoting everything to Sheldon nearly led to a devastating loss. Imagine pouring into somebody when your cup was never full; it is a recipe for disaster and chaos if I say so myself.

I realized passion transcends relationships, extending into daily rituals like connecting with nature or dedicating oneself wholeheartedly to endeavors. My family, particularly my grandparents' enduring love, provided a poignant illustration of profound passion—a love that surpassed challenges, inspiring my pursuit of enduring connections. Was that a part of making me want to stay, or was I just wrong about what love should be? Or was I just blinded by a vision falsely painted by a con artist who could lie through his teeth like it was a full-time job?

Work, an arena I entered, presented challenges in reconciling personal life with professional pursuits. A critical juncture forced a choice between a relationship I cherished and a career I deeply valued. This dichotomy underscored the complexities of intertwining love and ambition. You see, it wasn't just about his abuse; it was how he started to make me feel about my profession, the very essence of who I was and what I meant to him. He tried to take everything from me, including my soul, but I refused to let him take anything else.

The separation between love and passion emerged as a nuanced revelation. For me, loyalty overshadowed mere affection. Passion and loyalty, when intertwined, elevated connections to a different plane, a space less prone to the inconstancy of fleeting emotions. I felt disrespected and betrayed, which is the very opposite of what loyalty feels like. Defining love became a journey—love for friends differed from romantic love, and the unwavering love from a dedicated parent stood distinct from the complexities of our romantic bonds. Enduring love transcends mere affection, yet even the strongest affection can hesitate in the face of impossible challenges. Dealing with Sheldon was my impossible challenge. A challenge with no solution.

Ultimately, navigating through the complexities of love, passion, and loyalty unveiled profound insights—each relationship, each passion, possessed its distinct details, and the journey to define and understand these particulars remained an ongoing pursuit to me. It was like my mind had started to become uncluttered, and my pain began to mature me. I was no longer operating with the 21-year-old woman who had met this man. I began to learn how to navigate my maturity and operate in it. This gave me power. Power, I did not even realize at the time I had.

CHAPTER 9

Dependency and Life-Altering Moments

Sometimes, we find ourselves entangled in the temptations of various fast-paced lifestyles—sex, alcohol, drugs, and partying—a transient escape from internal struggles. I've succumbed to these temptations in my journey, engaging in actions I'm not proud of. Yet, we are all humans, made up of mostly hydrogen, oxygen, carbon, nitrogen, regret, and sins.

The weight of my trauma and crucial life moments has placed a permanent footprint in my life's history. No matter how much therapy a girl has, I can never forget what I have endured. These push pins of life have pinned me in tight. Two pregnancies marked by uncertainty and fear left indelible marks on my soul. The first, with Daijon, unfolded amid financial instability and personal life disturbances, leading me to a heart-wrenching decision—abortion. The second, with Sheldon, underscored my reluctance to perpetuate a cycle of absent fathers. My thoughts ran rapidly: the last thing this world needs are more fatherless children. Both experiences instilled in me an abysmal understanding of consequences and the value of timing. I trust in God's plan, awaiting the moment when parenthood aligns with my mental and financial readiness. Although I struggled with things as a child, I want to ensure my offspring can enjoy the fruits of my labor. Something good must come out of all this, right.

Music has always been a form of therapy for me, allowing me to feel my emotions deeply, reminiscing on the good and bad days, connecting me to the artist, and reminding me I am not alone. Music is philosophical; it's like speaking a language that everyone understands. It's in the beat, the way you become Insync and move your feet. We begin to understand one another more. I am a musicophile, admiring the beats and lyrics that save me from my agony. Soon after the betrayal, I began to express my pain and emotions on paper, which soon became a song I could call my own. I could now label myself an artist, a bit primmer than a "Porn star." That is how my journey as an artist began, by trying to mend my broken heart through melodies, lyrics, and symphonies. Music has been a part of my healing, a constant refuge— a source of solace, expression, and transformation. From childhood drums to present-day creations, music transcends mere hobby; it embodies healing and connection. My journey as a musician empowers me to convert pain into art, resonating with others on a visceral level. Though misunderstood and doubted, I've learned to validate my own worth, dismantling barriers obstructing my path to self-realization.

Reflecting on past hardships, I recognize a metamorphosis within myself—a transition from vulnerability to resilience. I will not fail; I was built to survive in the coldest conditions. Walls erected as shields, guarding against further pain, sometimes manifest as aggression or defensiveness. Yet, among the commotion, I seek solace in therapy and self-awareness, navigating triggers with newfound tools and grace.

Hindsight illuminates missed opportunities for self-preservation. Post-Sheldon breakup, seeking solace in companionship backfired, leading to betrayal and further toxicity. I've since learned the value of solitude, self-compassion, and discernment in cultivating a sanctuary of peace. Every trial and every hardship has shaped me into the person I am today, serving a purpose greater than myself. We as humans need a purpose to truly live a fulfilling life; what is yours? The magical part of that question is that it's yours to decide.

Today, my foremost priority is safeguarding my peace—a hard-won treasure amidst life's commotion. I've learned the importance of boundaries, discernment, and self-protection. No longer naive, I recognize the gravity of potential harm, remaining vigilant in preserving my well-being on all fronts. In hindsight, the dangers loomed large; I count my blessings, acknowledging the potential for far graver consequences.

In this journey of self-preservation, I've emerged stronger, wiser, and fiercely protective of my inner sanctum. Each challenge and setback have fortified my resolve to live authentically, unapologetically, and with purpose. Once veiled, my eyes now perceive the world with clarity, guided by an unwavering commitment to my well-being and growth. My spiritual guides and ancestors are always at work, and fortunately for me, they don't need lunch breaks.

⋄⊸◇◇◇◇◇◇◇◇◇◇◇◇◇◇◇◇◇◇◇◇⊸⋄

CHAPTER 10

Embracing Freedom and Self-Discovery

Section 1: Intangible Warfare

I am spiritually, physically, and mentally a free woman now. Spirituality saved me from the spiritual power struggle. I did not even know I was fighting; it was pure absurdity. How is one supposed to win a war without preparing for battle? I did not even know the true power of my opponent; he was a Trojan horse, a master of true deception and foolery. I strived to continue the endless journey of discovering myself. Figuring out who Victorya is, what she likes, and everything that encompasses her. Victorya is not an Alius; it is my real name, given to me the day I was born. Victorya, or Vicky whatever you want to call her who was once only known as an onlyfans girl, is now a published author, artist, demon slayer, and overcomer of all things that stand in her way. My previous relationships shaped me into how and what they wanted or needed me to do or look like. Finally, it's my time to be who I want to be, doing what I want to do. The bondage has been broken; I am free at last.

I am developing into the woman that I want to be. It was a learning experience in the most prominent years of my life, 18-24 years old, learning and holding down so much responsibility within the external environments with social media and my internal world. Although Sheldon has left physically, my lawyer and the FBI won't let me forget how much of a menace he is to society. My lawyer even mentioned that the next time I get into a relationship, he will screen their background check for me for free. That is sweet, considering I've spent hundreds of thousands of dollars for the love of law and order. Big bank takes little bank; ask both my exes. While others were in school or partying, I built my empire and legacy with occasional therapy sessions and phone calls with my lawyer. I'll admit I still don't have it all figured out; I am learning as I go, but my mindset is clear and on a healthy path. It really is mind over matter. I am content in knowing I can live life for me. I don't have to tolerate anything not for my greatest good. I don't have to kiss a man's ass unless I want to; we all know I'm a bit freaky. Certain people, unfortunately, don't have a choice and must tolerate certain things and lifestyles to have financial stability.

Currently, I am most proud of having spiritual awareness. Prayer, faith, tuning into my highest self, calculating my next move, and cognizance on all levels. I am growing in every possible way. I am an empath; I feel things deeply. It's truly a gift and curse. I have learned that energy transfers; even when someone hugs you, they give you, their energy. So, if I am negative all day, crying, etc., and I hug someone happy and fulfilled, I can feed off their energy through touch or a hug. It's like a battery; I would need to be charged, and they are complete.

Once you come to terms with the fact that life is all about frequency and energy, you don't take things personally, which is liberating. Understanding that certain people just vibrate at a lower frequency explains a lot. Another example is when you walk into a room and feel the tension; that is energy. With that in mind, I am more conscious than ever of whom I am near, who I speak to, and who I touch. I don't have to surround myself with negative, toxic, low-vibrating people. I used to hang around anyone and do anything. The selective approach is vital for me these days. Only some are in tune with the energy of others. Once you know, you know.

My biggest motivation is my little sister. When she looks at me, I want her to have a role model that she can admire and be proud of. I want to establish a good perspective of what a healthy relationship should be, how a man is supposed to treat a woman, and how to be her own person and not depend on anyone else. Sure, my occupation isn't the most outstanding example for her, but that doesn't mean I am not a good person. I can influence her and help her in other aspects of life. I want her to understand how powerful it is to be a strong woman. The history of a woman in society has changed. My mom, who was born in the 1960s, was raised to depend on what a man provides. That is just how it was back then. My financial independence stems from not wanting to ever depend on a man, or anyone, for that matter, the way my mother does. Don't get me wrong, I love my mother and my stepdad, but I promised you guys I would be honest. She instilled some things in me, and I am grateful for that. I only like to be in the kitchen and depend on a man when I role-play for my spicy videos.

The devil, Sheldon, motivated me to have more financial freedom. I deserve all the positive the world has to offer. Instead of always giving, I am finally ready to receive. I am ready to enter my "soft girl era." I accept Zelle, CashApp, Apple Pay", and wire transfers.

I have caught myself in a healing moment several times. Even writing this book has been cathartic. I've cried during some moments during this process, but in other moments when I would have cried, I didn't, and that shows me I have healed from that circumstance and trauma. Primarily, with me being the emotional person I am, it has been enlightening to notice how much more rational, understanding, and logical I am. I don't go 0-100 as I used to. The old Victorya would have snapped at people and not taken accountability. Self-reflection is monumental in my life today. I corrected my mistakes, as I still do wrongs, if that makes sense.

Years from now, I plan to build a generation of wealth for my children. It's imperative to me. I was passing down the legacy along with stability, something they can live with and work at to help their children. Not having that in my life, I lived through the struggle, and I don't want that life for them. They will know the dollar's value and not just be handed a golden spoon, but I don't want them to exert themselves to live, either. I want them to do what they are passionate about, not just work for financial abundance. I want to do more to help women, primarily in the adult entertainment industry, who have struggled with abuse. What and how has yet to be determined. I plan to return to school someday and obtain my finance degree; I only need a few credits. It would be a great accomplishment for me and my stepdad. I know he has always wanted that for me. He helped me in school and would sit with me for hours; he was so happy and proud every time I passed a test. I know our relationship has been rocky, but I am grateful that time is the most expensive gift you can give somebody.

My strength and reliance come from seeing my mom go through her life lessons. Everyone has their moments of not being the best role model. We have front-row seats to those occurrences; hopefully, someone will learn from them. I see she cannot be there for my sister all the time due to her own demons. That makes me want to be there even more—changing the narrative. I need to keep my head high and do more for all of us. I also want to prove that I am more than society paints me to be. Fuck society, assholes run the show, and validation comes with a hefty price tag. The only validation I have been seeking lately is internal.

Don't get me wrong, I still believe in love and hope to share moments with someone one day, but in a healthy way because I want to and choose to, and they choose me for who I am as my authentic self, not for the money, not for the social media fame just me. I want something genuine. When it happens, I will move slowly, not rush into anything, and take the time to get to know the other person. I will not shape myself into what the other person wants.

Whoever comes into my life must accept me in all my forms. That is someone I can build a future with. It's in God's hands. My primary focus is my healing journey, loving myself, expanding my self-awareness, creating my music, and finding freedom in expressing myself through it. It's dope how everything correlates in life; you must sit back and let the pieces fall together. Everything prepares you for the next step. Little did I know before, when I was younger, that I would make and write my music by playing the drums, making videos, and singing for the church choir. My passion began from an early age and now has flourished beyond my wildest dreams.

I have evolved from a victim to a hero and even a villain in some stories. I know myself; I live for myself and learn as I go. I will continue to protect my energy in all my endeavors. I am living my truth, pain, trauma, mistakes, and all. This is how we grow. I am proud of myself. I know who I am; no one can take that away. God has blessed me and will continue to do so as I continue to be me and live unapologetically in my truth and evolution.

I know I said some beautiful and motivational words of wisdom, but I must mention something. Don't judge me, but I had purchased an investment property with this asshole Sheldon. We are in an ugly legal battle for the property I paid for. Yes, I know I made a mistake, but we already went over that, and that's not the point. The point is the man is like a hemorrhoid. If you had him once, he would always return no matter how hard you tried to keep him away. I showed up with a few friends at the house, and it almost went down, but that's for the next book.

We live in a world of self-gratification. Appreciation may come off as self-centered and conceited. I am far from conceited and, on most days, quite the opposite; I am always dissatisfied and want more, fighting the feeling of not doing enough. Part of growing and adulting is not caring about people's opinions, so here I go...I first want to thank myself, yes me, Victorya. I want to thank myself for all the nights I wanted to give up, and I didn't. I thank myself for dragging myself out of bed and opening the curtains on my darkest days. I want to thank myself for numbing my heart so I can muster up the courage to work and continue with life. I want to thank myself for being my biggest fan and never backing down.

I don't give myself enough credit; I have been

through hell and back and came out alive, and hell is not one of the many wonders of the world; it's a cataclysm. When you can only depend on yourself financially, you don't have a choice; you must keep going. There is no other option, and there is no room for mistakes. I also want to thank my dearest family, friends, and fans who have helped me and spoke life into me. My mother, stepfather, Rob, Mel, and other close friends. There are not enough words to describe my gratitude. Thank you, and I hope you guys are proud of this new me!